THIS JOURNAL IS OVERDUE

ALA Editions

CHICAGO 2019

Edited by Jamie Santoro

With contributions from her creative colleagues: Rachel Chance, Rob Christopher, Terra Dankowski, Alejandra Diaz, Alison Elms, Peggy Galus, Samantha Imburgia, Phil Morehart, Jordan Sarti, Sanhita SinhaRoy, and Kimberly Thornton.

©2019 by the American Library Association

Extensive effort has gone into ensuring the reliability of the information in this book; however, the publisher makes no warranty, express or implied, with respect to the material contained herein.

ISBN: 978-0-8389-1777-0 (paper)

Book design by Kim Thornton in the Freight Text Pro and Violina Rough typefaces. Cover illustration © Feralchildren/Adobe Stock. Interior illustrations © KatyaKatya/Adobe Stock.

♾ This paper meets the requirements of ANSI/NISO Z39.48-1992 (Permanence of Paper).

Printed in the United States of America

23 22 21 20 19   5 4 3 2 1

A LETTER TO

LIBRARY LOVERS

Dear Writer, Reader, and Lover of Libraries and Books,

Welcome to *This Journal Is Overdue*. In these pages, you will find a hearty dose of writing prompts about favorite characters, engaging plots, and memorable stories. Each of these prompts is designed to spur your imagination and help you hone your skills as a writer so jump right in, tap your imagination, unleash your creativity, and rewrite your favorite fairy tale. Most of all, Enjoy!

Your Friends at the American Library Association

Imagine you have been invited to dinner with your favorite author.
What question would you ask before you even had a chance
to look at the menu? Write the dialogue.

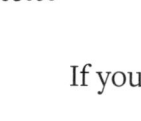

If your library had a mascot, what would it be? Why?
Draw it.

· · · · · · · · · · · · · · · · ·

Who is your fictional BFF? Why?

_____

_____

_____

_____

_____

_____

_____

_____

_____

_____

Pull a book off the shelf. Use the words in the title
in the first sentence of a story.

(continued) →

Imagine your library as the setting for a reality TV show, drama, or cartoon. Write a summary of the first episode.

List 5 books you wish
had sequels.

1) _____

_____

2) _____

_____

3) _____

_____

4) _____

_____

5) _____

_____

List 5 books you are dying to read
based on their covers.

1) _____

_____

2) _____

_____

3) _____

_____

4) _____

_____

5) _____

_____

List 5 books that would
make good films.

1) _____

2) _____

3) _____

4) _____

5) _____

List 5 favorite films adapted
from books.

1) _____

2) _____

3) _____

4) _____

5) _____

Write a story inspired by Edvard Munch's "The Scream."

Which character from a book would you most like to meet and why?

_____

_____

_____

_____

_____

Write a toast to your favorite fictional couple.

_____

_____

_____

_____

_____

_____

Who is your favorite bad boy/girl of literature? The one you love to hate?
Why do you despise him/her so much?

_____

_____

_____

_____

_____

_____

Write a love letter to a fictional old flame.

If you could give Romeo and Juliet advice, what would it be?

Your life is a book. Write your acknowledgments.

Rewrite a fairy tale. Give it a surprise ending
or an interesting twist.

_____

_____

_____

_____

_____

_____

_____

_____

_____

_____

_____

_____

_____

_____

_____

_____

_____

_____

_____

_____

_____

_____

_____

_____

(continued) ⟶

Write a story that includes these words: barbaric, bloodlust, bibliophile.

Write a short story inspired by this line from *Wuthering Heights* by Emily Brontë:
"Terror made me cruel."

Pull a book off the shelf, read the back cover, then take a go
at writing an opening paragraph to the book.

_____

_____

_____

_____

_____

_____

_____

_____

Which of your friends would make a great character in a book and why?

_____

_____

_____

_____

_____

_____

_____

_____

_____

Write a story about a conversation you overheard.

Write your list of errands
as a poem.

Write a list of interview questions for
someone real or fictional.

Interviewee: _____

Open a book to the last page. Find the last line and make it
the first line of your writing today.

(continued) →

Fast Forward: Take any novel you've read over the past year and write an epilogue. What happens to the characters in 5 years?

In 10 years?

Choose a literary classic that is widely acclaimed and beloved
by generations of readers and write a scathing review
arguing the book is overrated.

_____

. . . .

Write a tribute to someone you regard as a hero.

_____

Write a dystopia about your hometown.

(continued) ➔

Write your own fake news story.

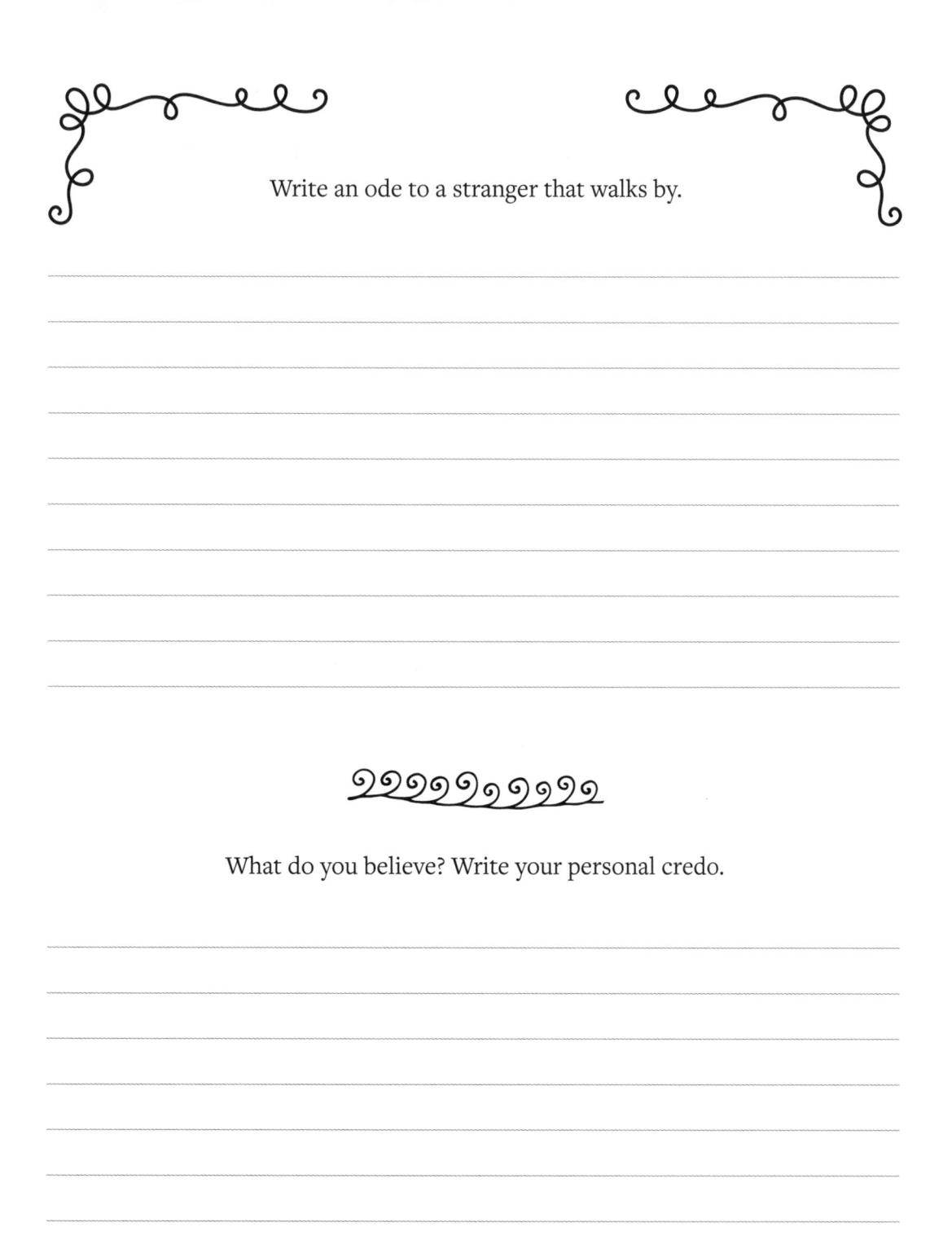

Write an ode to a stranger that walks by.

_____

_____

_____

_____

_____

_____

_____

_____

What do you believe? Write your personal credo.

_____

_____

_____

_____

_____

_____

_____

_____

_____

Last night, Ms. Peacock murdered Mr. Plum with a candlestick in the library. Reconstruct both characters' movements in the hours leading up to the crime and reveal what led Ms. Peacock and Mr. Plum to that fateful moment.

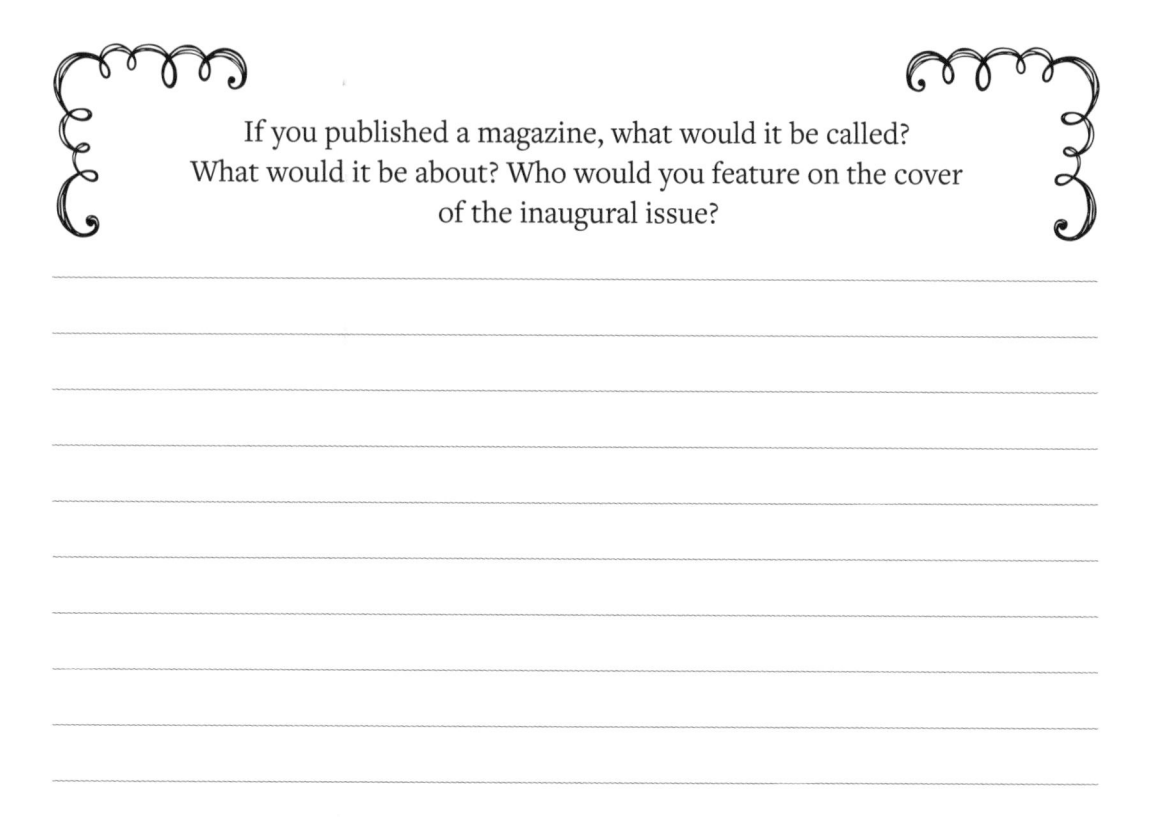

If you published a magazine, what would it be called?
What would it be about? Who would you feature on the cover
of the inaugural issue?

Describe your day in words by creating your own word cloud.

What 5 books made you laugh?

1) _____

2) _____

3) _____

4) _____

5) _____

What 5 books made you cry?

1) _____

2) _____

3) _____

4) _____

5) _____

What 5 books do you love to hate?

1) _____

2) _____

3) _____

4) _____

5) _____

What 5 books do you refuse to read?

1) _____

2) _____

3) _____

4) _____

5) _____

"A shrill cry came from the stacks. It was . . ."
Complete the sentence and finish the scene.

Write a table of contents for your life up to this point

Write a poem about a secret you know. Write it in such a way as to keep the secret a secret.

Write about an imaginary journey you'd like to take.

Write a humorous lament about something you have lost.

Pitch a new mockumentary.

You're a superhero! What's your name and superpower?
Tell your story and draw your emblem.

Name: _____

Superpower: _____

Write a love story that ends badly.

Think of a fictional character you'd like to date.
Write a note to that person to express your wish.

Write a pledge of allegiance to libraries.

Without using the words "I" or "me," write
the opening scene of your memoir.

Write a story using these stock characters: a capricious and malevolent ruler, a prince who is shirking his responsibilities, an old woman who lives deep in the forest.

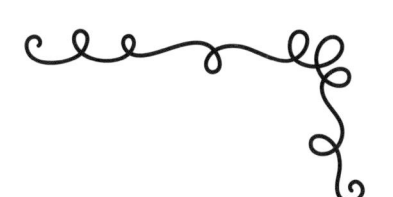

Write your own eulogy.

_____
_____
_____
_____
_____
_____
_____
_____
_____

Your life is now a best-selling book. Write the copy for the back cover.

_____
_____
_____
_____
_____
_____
_____
_____
_____

Write the lyrics to an indie rock song. Include a trip to Portland, a deck of playing cards, and a girl named Sylvia.

_____

_____

_____

_____

_____

_____

_____

_____

_____

_____

_____

_____

_____

_____

_____

_____

_____

_____

_____

_____

Think about one of your favorite books. Make a list of 10 reasons why your friends should read it.

Book: _____

_____

1) _____

_____

2) _____

_____

3) _____

_____

4) _____

_____

5) _____

_____

6) _____

_____

7) _____

_____

8) _____

_____

9) _____

_____

10) _____

_____

Write the opening scene of a murder mystery set in your hometown.

What book have you hidden from onlookers? Why did you hide it?

_____

_____

_____

_____

_____

What current book do you think will be read 100 years from now. Why?

_____

_____

_____

_____

_____

If you could go back in time and give yourself some advice,
what would you say?

_____

_____

_____

_____

_____

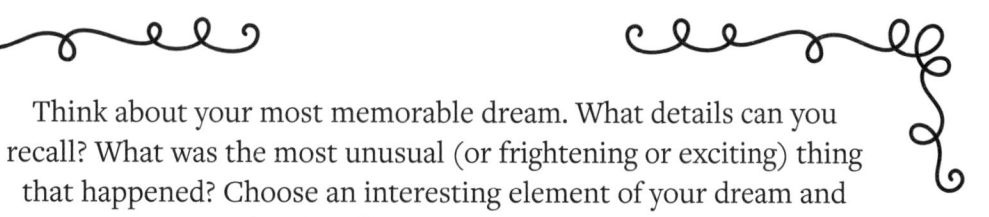

Think about your most memorable dream. What details can you recall? What was the most unusual (or frightening or exciting) thing that happened? Choose an interesting element of your dream and develop that into a short story.

Write a letter to a favorite main character.

Now, write the character's reply.

Write a short biography of your mother.

_____

_____

_____

_____

_____

_____

_____

_____

_____

_____

_____

Write a short biography of your father.

_____

_____

_____

_____

_____

_____

_____

_____

_____

_____

_____

_____

Write a short story inspired by this line from *Of Mice and Men* by John Steinbeck: "Maybe ever'body in the whole damn world is scared of each other."

Think about an incident in your life and turn it into a tall tale.

Update a character from a book set in the past.
What would he/she be wearing/doing/saying today?

Which 5 fictional characters do you secretly envy?

1) _____

2) _____

3) _____

4) _____

5) _____

List 5 possible titles for your autobiography.

1) _____

2) _____

3) _____

4) _____

5) _____

What 5 phobias do you think would make a great plot twist for a book?

1) _____

2) _____

3) _____

4) _____

5) _____

List 5 phrases you would teach your pet parrot.

1) _____

2) _____

3) _____

4) _____

5) _____

Write a ballad or song about the characters and events
in a book you just read. Include a catchy refrain.

_____

_____

_____

_____

_____

_____

_____

_____

_____

Write an acrostic poem using the letters in the title of a book
or the name of a character or author.

_____

_____

_____

_____

_____

_____

_____

_____

Write a short story inspired by this line from *The Road* by
Cormac McCarthy: "You forget what you want to remember,
and you remember what you want to forget."

Write a story that includes these words: library, latte, and labyrinth.

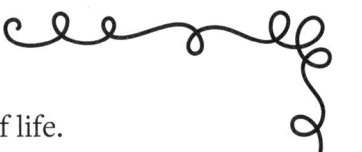

Write a treatise on the meaning of life.

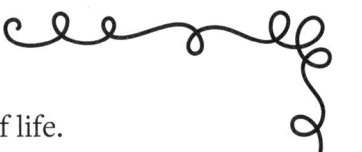

Give fashion advice to Lisbeth Salander (*The Girl with the Dragon Tattoo*).

Finish this scene: He approached the reference desk, looked stealthily around, and then handed the note to the librarian.

_____
_____
_____
_____
_____
_____
_____
_____
_____
_____

Write about writer's block.

_____
_____
_____
_____
_____
_____
_____
_____
_____
_____
_____
_____

Imagine the dialogue if Jane Eyre met James Bond.

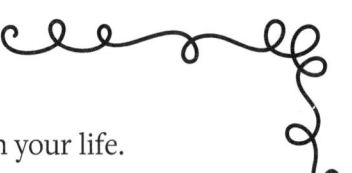

War and Peace: Write about a conflict in your life.

Write a short story inspired by this line from *Kafka on the Shore* by Haruki Murakami: "Memories warm you up from the inside. But they also tear you apart."

(continued) →

Create a conspiracy theory.

_____

_____

_____

_____

_____

Create and write about a ridiculous holiday.

_____

_____

_____

_____

_____

_____

You are stranded on an island with pen, paper, and a bottle.
Write a message in a bottle.

_____

_____

_____

_____

_____

_____

You have just stolen the only known copy of an award-winning chef's signature recipe. Write a ransom note demanding something in return.

Write a dystopian outline for a dystopian novel.

Catch 22: Write a story where there's no easy way out.

Write a short story inspired by this line from *The Mysterious Island* by Jules Verne: "It is a great misfortune to be alone, my friends; and it must be believed that solitude can quickly destroy reason."

Rant about a plot that disappointed.

•••••••••••••••

Write a magic spell.

1984: Set a scene in this year.

Pride and Prejudice: Write a story about an initial misunderstanding that set a relationship down the wrong path.

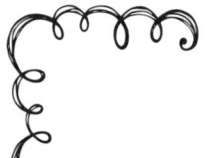

Write a letter from Lily Bart to Dear Abby
asking for advice on dating.

Now write Dear Abby's reply.

"The fugitive slipped into the library just before closing time."
What happens next? Write that story.

Write a review of the last movie you saw.

_____
_____
_____
_____
_____
_____
_____
_____
_____
_____

Write the acceptance speech you'll give when you win your Pulitzer.

_____
_____
_____
_____
_____
_____
_____
_____
_____
_____

The Republic: Write a short story about an ideal society.

Imagine the dialogue if Nancy Drew met Norman Bates.

Write a short story inspired by this line from *Don Quixote* by Miguel de Cervantes Saavedra: "Finally, from so little sleeping and so much reading, his brain dried up and he went completely out of his mind."

(continued) ⟶

Write a letter from Sylvia Plath to Dorothy Parker
asking for advice on how to save a marriage.

_____
_____
_____
_____
_____
_____
_____
_____
_____

Now write Dorothy Parker's reply.

_____
_____
_____
_____
_____
_____
_____
_____
_____

Great Expectations: Write a short story about an orphan named Pip, but set your tale in a small Midwestern town in the present day.

Things Fall Apart: Write a story about a character who makes a singular, catastrophic mistake that affects everything that happens next.

Harry Potter and the Sorcerer's Stone was rejected 12 times and J. K. Rowling was told "not to quit her day job." Write the 13th rejection letter.

•••••••••••••••

Summarize your life story to date in one paragraph.

Write a short story inspired by this line from *London Fields* by Martin Amis: "And meanwhile time goes about its immemorial work of making everyone look and feel like shit."

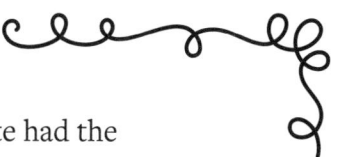

Imagine the dialogue if Truman Capote had the
opportunity to interview Voldemort.

Write a short story inspired by this line from *Revolutionary Road* by Richard Yates: "No one forgets the truth; they just get better at lying."

Write a short story about celebrity, bling, and narcissism.

•••••••••••••••

Write an apology that is **OVERDUE**.

_____
_____
_____
_____
_____
_____
_____
_____
_____
_____
_____

•••••••••••••••

Write a thank you that is **OVERDUE**.

_____
_____
_____
_____
_____
_____
_____
_____
_____
_____
_____

Write a story that includes these words: card catalog, cat, cacophony.

What is the most fitting cocktail to serve with your 5 favorite books?

Book:

1) _____

2) _____

3) _____

4) _____

5) _____

Drink:

1) _____

2) _____

3) _____

4) _____

5) _____

What 5 authors (dead or alive) would you invite to a dinner party?
What would each of them bring?

Author:

1) _____

2) _____

3) _____

4) _____

5) _____

Item:

1) _____

2) _____

3) _____

4) _____

5) _____

Create a travel brochure for the setting of the book you just read.

Book:

Location:

What's to love?

·······•·······••

Why go now?

··•······•····•••

What to pack?

What to do?

What to see?

Write about a day at work you'd like to forget.

_____
_____
_____
_____
_____
_____
_____
_____
_____
_____
_____
_____
_____
_____
_____
_____
_____
_____
_____
_____
_____
_____

Imagine that you are a time traveler. How are you able to move through time and space? Write a scene that describes your first adventure and the vehicle you used to get there.

•••••••••••••••••

Write 3 utterly ridiculous and hilarious satirical headlines (à la *The Onion*)
based on today's news.

1) _____

_____

2) _____

_____

3) _____

_____

•••••••••••••••••

What 3 questions would you ask your favorite fictional character?

1) _____

_____

2) _____

_____

3) _____

_____

•••••••••••••••••

What 3 questions would stump a reference librarian?

1) _____

_____

2) _____

_____

3) _____

_____

Write a short story inspired by this line from *Their Eyes Were Watching God* by Zora Neale Hurston: "She had waited all her life for something, and it had killed her when it found her."

(continued) ⟶

Write a letter from "Young Goodman Brown" to the Dalai Lama
asking for advice about Faith.

_____

_____

_____

_____

_____

_____

_____

_____

_____

Now write the Dalai Lama's reply.

_____

_____

_____

_____

_____

_____

_____

_____

_____

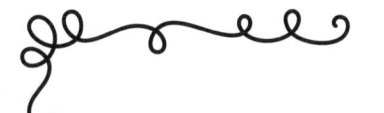

Write a story that includes these words:
archives, acrimonious, augur.

Pen the outline to a fantasy novel. What sort of magic, mythical creatures, or supernatural elements will you include?

Come up with 5 alternatives to this literary catchphrase from the miserly Scrooge in Charles Dickens's classic story, *A Christmas Carol*: "Bah! Humbug!"

1) _____

2) _____

3) _____

4) _____

5) _____

Come up with 5 alternatives to this literary catchphrase from Rhett Butler in Margaret Mitchell's novel, *Gone with the Wind*: "Frankly, my dear, I don't give a damn."

1) _____

2) _____

3) _____

4) _____

5) _____

Imagine the dialogue if Hannibal Lecter met Hermione Granger.

Pick an era and setting, and then pen an outline
for a historical novel.

Who would you cast in a movie based on your life?

Cast:

Character:

Create a soundtrack for your biopic.

Song:

Artist:

Write a dating profile as one of your favorite characters.

Character Name:

Other than appearance, what is the first thing that people notice about you?

What's the most important thing you're looking for in another person?

What are your three best life skills?

1)

2)

3)

How do you typically spend your leisure time?

_____
_____
_____
_____
_____

What are 5 things you can't live without?

1) _____
2) _____
3) _____
4) _____
5) _____

What are your favorite books, movies, shows, music, and food?

_____
_____
_____
_____
_____
_____
_____

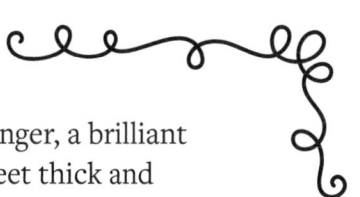

Write a tall tale that features a swaggering stranger, a brilliant protagonist, and a rattlesnake that is "two feet thick and thirty feet long."

Dream up 5 alternative titles for . . .

The Great Gatsby

1) _____
_____

2) _____
_____

3) _____
_____

4) _____
_____

5) _____
_____

Lincoln in the Bardo

1) _____
_____

2) _____
_____

3) _____
_____

4) _____
_____

5) _____
_____

The Road

1) _____
_____

2) _____
_____

3) _____
_____

4) _____
_____

5) _____
_____

Heart of Darkness

1) _____
_____

2) _____
_____

3) _____
_____

4) _____
_____

5) _____
_____

Write a letter from Captain Ahab to Lady Macbeth in which he shares his plans for revenge.

_____

_____

_____

_____

_____

_____

_____

_____

_____

Now write Lady Macbeth's reply.

_____

_____

_____

_____

_____

_____

_____

_____

_____

_____

Write the start to a Western romance. Include cowboys, American Indians, bandits, lawmen, bounty hunters, outlaws, soldiers.

List 5 unusual names for characters in a . . .

Western

1) _____

2) _____

3) _____

4) _____

5) _____

Romance

1) _____

2) _____

3) _____

4) _____

5) _____

Fantasy

1) _____

2) _____

3) _____

4) _____

5) _____

Historical Fiction novel

1) _____

2) _____

3) _____

4) _____

5) _____

Write a poem using these homophones: bizarre, bazaar, pray, prey, profit, prophet.

Write a poem using these homophones: guessed, guest, gorilla, guerilla, loot, lute.

Write a story that includes these words:
reference desk, raconteur, retribution.

Write an imaginary story about your ancestors.

Write a story about an endearing troublemaker.

Pen 5 alternative titles for . . .

A Heartbreaking Work of Staggering Genius

1) _____

2) _____

3) _____

4) _____

5) _____

Everything Is Illuminated

1) _____

2) _____

3) _____

4) _____

5) _____

Looking for Alaska

1) _____

2) _____

3) _____

4) _____

5) _____

A Good Man Is Hard to Find

1) _____

2) _____

3) _____

4) _____

5) _____

Write a story inspired by Vincent Van Gogh's "Starry Night."

Think of an author you'd like to have dinner with. Pen a note that might convince him or her to join you.

_____
_____
_____
_____
_____
_____
_____
_____
_____
_____
_____

•••••••••••••••••

Gone with the Wind by Margaret Mitchell was rejected 38 times before it was published. Write the 39th rejection letter.

_____
_____
_____
_____
_____
_____
_____
_____

Write a short story inspired by this line from *Frankenstein* by Mary Shelley:
"Nothing is so painful to the human mind as a great and sudden change."

•••••••••••••••••

Think of a favorite book. Write
a poem that sums up the story.

_____
_____
_____
_____
_____
_____
_____
_____
_____
_____
_____
_____
_____
_____
_____
_____
_____
_____
_____
_____
_____

•••••••••••••••••

Write 5 Tweets you will
never send.

@_____
_____
_____
_____

@_____
_____
_____
_____

@_____
_____
_____
_____

@_____
_____
_____
_____

@_____
_____
_____
_____

Make a list of alphabetical advice that Holden Caulfield might give to Scout Finch.

Now make a list of alphabetical advice that Scout Finch might give to Holden Caulfield.

•••••••••••••••

What are 3 terrible ideas for a science fiction novel?

1) _____

_____

2) _____

_____

3) _____

_____

•••••••••••••••

Write 3 unexpected fortunes you'd like to find in a fortune cookie.

1) _____

_____

2) _____

_____

3) _____

_____

•••••••••••••••

What are 3 ideas for a new reality show that will never be produced?

1) _____

_____

2) _____

_____

3) _____

_____

Write a story inspired by Grant Wood's "American Gothic."

Invent 5 curse words to use in a
novel about rebellious teenagers.

1) _____

_____

2) _____

_____

3) _____

_____

4) _____

_____

5) _____

_____

What 5 fictional characters would make
a great President of the United States?

1) _____

_____

2) _____

_____

3) _____

_____

4) _____

_____

5) _____

_____

What 5 characters would make the
best road trip companions?

1) _____

_____

2) _____

_____

3) _____

_____

4) _____

_____

5) _____

_____

What 5 biographies would you
like to write?

1) _____

_____

2) _____

_____

3) _____

_____

4) _____

_____

5) _____

_____

Write a love letter that is **OVERDUE**.

_____
_____
_____
_____
_____
_____
_____
_____
_____
_____
_____

Write an office memo that is **OVERDUE**.

_____
_____
_____
_____
_____
_____
_____
_____
_____
_____
_____

Write a story inspired by Diego Rivera's "The Flower Carrier."

Write a short story inspired by this line from *Great Expectations* by Charles Dickens:
"We need never be ashamed of our tears."

(continued) ⟶

Choose one of your favorite fictional characters and write a speculative piece about the character's childhood that might help explain why the character acts as she does.

Write a humorous list of all the things you were supposed to do today that you are NOT going to do, and why.

Pen a lullaby for Antoine de Saint-Exupéry's *The Little Prince*.

Write a new adventure for Eloise, the mischievous little girl
who lives at The Plaza Hotel.

Write the start to a horror story about a science experiment
that goes terribly, terribly wrong.

Draft 5 alternative titles for . . .

White Noise

1) _____
_____

2) _____
_____

3) _____
_____

4) _____
_____

5) _____
_____

Manhattan Beach

1) _____
_____

2) _____
_____

3) _____
_____

4) _____
_____

5) _____
_____

A Visit from the Goon Squad

1) _____
_____

2) _____
_____

3) _____
_____

4) _____
_____

5) _____
_____

Charlotte's Web

1) _____
_____

2) _____
_____

3) _____
_____

4) _____
_____

5) _____
_____

Write the lyrics to a country song.
Include a truck, a heartbreak, and
an old hound dog.

Write a bucket list for your
favorite book character.

Write a short story about the perfect crime.

Write a letter to your literary doppelganger.